~~DAD~~ MOM JOKES

Cause moms are funny too

"If I can make one person laugh long enough to forget their problems, then my day was not wasted."

—Unknown—

TABLE OF CONTENTS

FROM THE AUTHOR	PAGE 7
THE BEST JOKES EVER	PAGE 9
EVERYDAY JOKES	PAGE 11
VALENTINE'S DAY JOKES	PAGE 135
ST. PATRICK'S DAY JOKES	PAGE 143
EASTER JOKES	PAGE 151
DERBY INSPIRED JOKES	PAGE 157
U.S.A. INSPIRED JOKES	PAGE 165
HALLOWEEN JOKES	PAGE 173
THANKSGIVING JOKES	PAGE 187
CHRISTMAS JOKES	PAGE 195
MY JOKES	PAGE 209

FROM THE AUTHOR

Hello, my name is Jaclyn and I am the mother of a beautiful girl named Peyton. We are from Louisville, KY in the United States of America.

Peyton is six years old at the time this book was written. She loves jokes, but still gives me the eyeroll many times when I share them with her. However, I have inspired her to create and share her own jokes with others. She is always coming up with the silliest things, but loves to make other people smile! I have no doubt she will carry on sharing jokes and/or laughs for as long as she lives.

I have been a fan of corny "dad" jokes for as long as I can remember. I love hearing them and telling them! Sharing a laugh is one of the easiest ways we can connect with other people. I have been wanting to write a book for a long time to make it easier to keep up with all the jokes I have enjoyed over the years. I wanted to make it a point that moms can be funny too and these jokes aren't just for dads.

All jokes within this book are jokes I've heard, shared, and told myself. I cannot take credit for the creation of any joke; I can only take credit for saving them and sharing them with you.

This book is full of jokes that are appropriate for people of all ages! Enjoy reading and sharing all the jokes!

There is a page with a chart dedicated for you to write in the page numbers of your favorite jokes for easy reference. I also included some blank pages at the end for you to write in your own jokes!

TIP: If you don't understand a joke right away, try saying it out loud.

THE BEST JOKES EVER

PAGE:	PAGE:	PAGE:	PAGE:	PAGE:	PAGE:
PAGE:	PAGE:	PAGE:	PAGE:	PAGE:	PAGE:
PAGE:	PAGE:	PAGE:	PAGE:	PAGE:	PAGE:
PAGE:	PAGE:	PAGE:	PAGE:	PAGE:	PAGE:
PAGE:	PAGE:	PAGE:	PAGE:	PAGE:	PAGE:
PAGE:	PAGE:	PAGE:	PAGE:	PAGE:	PAGE:
PAGE:	PAGE:	PAGE:	PAGE:	PAGE:	PAGE:
PAGE:	PAGE:	PAGE:	PAGE:	PAGE:	PAGE:
PAGE:	PAGE:	PAGE:	PAGE:	PAGE:	PAGE:
PAGE:	PAGE:	PAGE:	PAGE:	PAGE:	PAGE:

What did the blanket say when it fell off the bed?

"Oh sheet!"

What do you call an alligator wearing a vest?

An investigator!

What did the zero say to the eight?

"I like your belt!"

●·······●···●··● 👓 ●··●···●···●··●

Where do bad rainbows go?

They go to prism.

It's a light sentence; just enough time for them to reflect.

I would love to get paid to sleep!

It could be my dream job!

●·・●··●·・●·· 👓 ●·・●··●·・●··●

What do you call a snake wearing a hard hat?

A boa constructor!

●·・●··●·・●·· 👓 ●·・●··●·・●··●

I threw an iPhone into the lake the other day...

It's still syncing.

●·・●··●·・●·· 👓 ●·・●··●·・●··●

What kind of train likes to eat?

A chew chew train!

What did the father buffalo say when his son left for college?

"Bi-son!"

• • • • • • • • • • • 👓 • • • • • • • • • • •

Not all math puns are bad...

Just sum!

• • • • • • • • • • • 👓 • • • • • • • • • • •

Acupuncture is a jab well done!

• • • • • • • • • • • 👓 • • • • • • • • • • •

What is an avocado's favorite music?

Guac and Roll!

What is a big dog's favorite pastry?

A great danish!

If a short psychic broke out of jail...

you would have a small medium at large.

Why can't you trust a hotel receptionist?

Because they are always checking people out!

What do you get from a pampered cow?

Spoiled milk!

Why did the chicken cross the playground?

To get to the other slide!

Did you hear about the two antennas that got married?

The ceremony was only okay, but the reception was great!

When does a joke become a dad/mom joke?

When it becomes apparent!

What's the best part about living in Switzerland?

I'm not sure, but their flag is a big plus!

Why don't people sympathize when your books fall to the floor?

Because you only have your shelf to blame.

Did you hear about the world's biggest pickle?

Apparently it's a big dill.

Why didn't the melons get married?

Because they cantaloupe!

A guy was thrown in jail for refusing to take a nap!

Apparently he was resisting a rest.

Two people walk into a bar...

You would think the second one would have seen it there!

Why do fish live in salt water?

Because pepper water makes them sneeze!

Why are libraries so strict?

Because they have to go by the book!

How do you make an egg laugh?

You tell it a funny yolk!

What do you call a belt made of watches?

A waist of time!

• • • • • • • • • • •  • • • • • • • • • • •

What did the teacher do with her student's history report on cheese?

She grated it!

• • • • • • • • • • •  • • • • • • • • • • •

I once stayed up all night trying to figure out where the sun went.

Then, it dawned on me...

• •

Why do ducks have feathers?

To cover their butt quack!

What do you call a Labrador that becomes a magician?

A Labracadabrador!

•·•··•··•·•• 👓 •·•··•·•··•·••

What kind of music do chiropractors love?

Hip-pop!

•·•··•··•·•• 👓 •·•··•·•··•·••

What is a computer's favorite beat?

An algorhythm!

•·•··•··•·•• 👓 •·•··•·•··•·••

I wanted to post a joke about sodium...

But I was like Na, people won't get it.

The wedding was so beautiful even the cake was in tiers!

What does a nosey pepper do?

It gets jalapeño business!

What's the best way to determine how heavy a pepper is?

Give it a weigh, give it a weigh, give it a weigh now!

Why is running with bag pipes a bad idea?

Because you could put an aye out or better yet, get kilt!

Autocorrect is always making me say things
I didn't Nintendo!

Do you think mountains are funny?

Personally, I think they're hill areas!

Went to a Mary Poppins themed restaurant
the other day.

They had...
Super cauliflower cheese, but the lobster
was atrocious!

What I if told you...

You read the top line wrong.

Why shouldn't you become vegan?

Because it would be a big missed steak!

●·•··•··•·•● 👓 ●··•··•··•·•●

It's a wonder how stadiums get so hot when they're filled with fans!

●·•··•··•·•● 👓 ●··•··•··•·•●

Why did the peanut file a police report?

Because he was a salted!

●·•··•··•·•● 👓 ●··•··•··•·•●

Did you know...
You can distinguish between an Alligator and a Crocodile by paying attention to whether the animal sees you later or in a while.

What's orange and sounds like a parrot?

A carrot!

• • • • • • • • • • • 👓 • • • • • • • • • • • •

What kind of shoes do frogs wear?

Open toad!

• • • • • • • • • • • 👓 • • • • • • • • • • • •

How do birds learn to fly?

They just wing it!

• • • • • • • • • • • 👓 • • • • • • • • • • • •

Parallel lines have so much in common, it's a shame they'll never meet!

What kind of nut is the richest?

A Cashew!

Why does Humpty Dumpty love Autumn?

Because he had a great fall!

Can a kangaroo jump higher than a house?

Of course! Houses can't jump!

Whoever invented knock knock jokes should get a no-bell prize!

People think being a server isn't a respectable job.

But it puts food on the table.

Did you know that bats are not actually blind?

That's why they're so good at hitting baseballs!

How do you keep warm in a cold room?

You go to the corner because it's always 90°!

What do you call a cow after she gives birth?

Decaf!

I just purchased a new dry-erase board.

It's remarkable!

••••••••••••• 👓 ••••••••••••••

What's a computer's least favorite food?

Spam!

•••••••••••••• 👓 ••••••••••••••

My friend writes lyrics about sewing machines.

She's a Singer-songwriter!

•••••••••••••• 👓 ••••••••••••••

Who designed King Arthur's round table?

Sir cumference!

There's a fine line between a numerator and a denominator.

Only a fraction of people will find this funny.

"Dad/mom, are we pyromaniacs?"

"Yes, we arson."

My friend claims I'm the cheapest person they have ever met!

I'm not buying it.

I got a new job at a prison library.

It has pros and cons.

With great power comes a huge electricity bill!

• • • • • • • • • • 👓 • • • • • • • • • • •

If you want to open a store, I recommend selling stoves.

You'll immediately offer a range of hot products!

• • • • • • • • • • 👓 • • • • • • • • • • •

"Orion's belt is a big waist of space!"

Terrible joke, only three stars.

• • • • • • • • • • 👓 • • • • • • • • • • •

How does a tree access the internet?

It logs in!

I wonder if the Earth makes fun of the moon for having no life.

What did the momma cow say to the baby cow?

It's pasture bedtime!

Did you know milk is the fastest liquid on Earth?

It's pasteurized before you even see it!

• • • • • • • • • • • • 👓 • • • • • • • • • • • •

What did one wall say to the other wall?

"Let's meet in the corner!"

Why does the coffee taste like mud?

Because it was ground just a couple minutes ago!

●··●···●··●··● 👓 ●··●···●··●··●

Why don't polar bears get married?

Because they always have cold feet!

●··●···●··●··● 👓 ●··●···●··●··●

Today at the bank, an old lady asked if I could check her balance.

So I pushed her over.

●··●···●··●··● 👓 ●··●···●··●··●

Why did the banker switch careers?

She lost interest.

Scientists recently discovered a new dinosaur that's very intelligent!

It's called Thesaurus!

What did the tree say to the lumberjack?

I'm falling for you.

A photon checks into a hotel.

The bellhop asks, "Can I help you with your luggage?"

The photon replies, "I don't have any because I'm traveling light!"

How do you make an elephant float?

Two scoops of ice cream, one can of root beer, and an elephant!

Where do typists go for a drink?

The space bar!

•·•··•·•··• 👓 •··•·•··•·•·•

What's Al Gore's favorite kind of math?

Algorithms!

•·•··•·•··• 👓 •··•·•··•·•·•

Which is correct?

"The yolk of the egg are white." or "The yolk of the egg is white."

Neither! The yolk of the egg is yellow!

•·•··•·•··• 👓 •··•·•··•·•·•

What is a sea monster's favorite snack?

Ships and dip!

Why is Peter Pan always flying?

Because he can never never land!

• • • • • • • • • • 👓 • • • • • • • • • • •

Why can't you trust an atom?

Because they make up literally everything!

• • • • • • • • • • 👓 • • • • • • • • • • •

Did you hear the joke about the roof?

I would tell you, but it tends to go over people's heads.

• • • • • • • • • • 👓 • • • • • • • • • • •

What do you call a bird whose always on business trips?

A frequent flyer!

If you ever find yourself addicted to the Hokey Pokey, don't worry.

You can always turn yourself around!

Did you hear about the quarry that went out of business?

They hit rock bottom!

A woman once said she recognized me from a vegetarian club...

But I've never met herbivore.

Did you hear about the two thieves that stole the calendar?

They each got six months!

Have you heard about the frog that was raised by bunnies?

All he can say is "rabbit"

• • • • • • • • • • • 👓 • • • • • • • • • • •

What happens when a frog's car breaks down?

It gets toad!

• • • • • • • • • • • 👓 • • • • • • • • • • •

Shapes are cool.

But I think circles are pointless.

• • • • • • • • • • • 👓 • • • • • • • • • • •

What happened to the plant in math class?

It grew square roots!

What do clouds wear under their shorts?

Thunderpants!

Never try to annoy someone with bird puns.

Because toucan play that game!

What is the best way to carve wood?

Whittle by whittle.

⬤·⬤···⬤···⬤··⬤ 👓 ⬤··⬤···⬤···⬤··⬤

Why was the leopard so bad at hide and seek?

No matter where she hid, she was always spotted!

Which playing cards are the best dancers?

The King and Queen of clubs!

•·•··•··•·•• 👓 ••·•··•··•·••

Apparently no one knows why Notre Dame caught fire...

But Quasimodo has a hunch.

•·•··•··•·•• 👓 ••·•··•··•·••

Why did the school kids eat their homework?

Because their teacher told them it was a piece of cake!

•·•··•··•·•• 👓 ••·•··•··•·••

A neutron walks into a bar and asks the bartender, "How much for a drink?"

Bartender says, "For you, no charge!"

A five dollar bill walks into a bar...

Bartender says, "You can't be here. It's singles night!"

How do billboards talk?

They use sign language!

I once did a theatrical performance about puns.

It was a play on words.

How much does a pirate pay for corn?

A buccaneer!

What do you call a cold canine?

A chili dog!

Did you know the first French fries weren't cooked in France?

They were actually cooked in Greece!

I always thought going to see a chiropractor was a waste of time...

But I stand corrected.

•·•··•··•·•• 👓 •·•··•·•··•··••

I applied to be a pilot, but I couldn't land the job.

Why did the physics teacher break up with the biology teacher?

Because they had no chemistry!

What's Forrest Gump's password?

1forrest1

How does our solar system keep it's pants up?

With an asteroid belt!

Why wouldn't the shrimp share his treasure?

Because he's shellfish!

What is a deer's favorite dance?

The doe-si-doe!

———

Why does the mushroom always like to party?

Because he is a fungi!

———

Which animal is the least trustworthy?

Cheetahs!

———

What do you call a shoe made out of a banana?

A slipper!

What do you call a bear with no teeth?

A gummy bear!

Why do cows have bells?

Because their horns don't work!

How many tickles does it take to make an octopus laugh?

Ten-tickles!

How do you organize a space party?

You planet!

What do you call a fat psychic?

A four-chin teller!

•••••••••••• 👓 ••••••••••••

Why did the cookie go to the hospital?

Because he felt crummy!

•••••••••••• 👓 ••••••••••••

What do you call a crate full of ducks?

A box of quackers!

•••••••••••• 👓 ••••••••••••

What do you call a fake noodle?

An im-pasta!

What kind of bird sticks to sweaters?

A vel-crow!

What do dinosaurs pay with?

Tyrannosaurus Checks!

Did you know "t-shirt" stands for "Tyrannosaurus Shirt?"

It's because it has short arms!

•••••••••••• 👓 ••••••••••••

What do you call someone who sells themselves for spaghetti?

A pastatute!

What is a ratchet girl's favorite store in the mall?

Thot Topic!

• • • • • • • • • • • 👓 • • • • • • • • • • •

What does a grizzly say when he calls customer service?

"Just bear with me."

What did the Power Ranger say to his patients when he became a doctor?

"It's morphine time!"

Why do cows have hooves instead of feet?

Because they lac-tose!

What did the car say to it's tires?

"Thanks for keeping it wheel!"

●•●••●••●••● 👓 ●••●••●••●••●

What kind of class does a coal miner take?

Minecrafts!

●•●••●••●••● 👓 ●••●••●••●••●

What did the salt say to the pepper?

"Catch you next seasoning!"

●•●••●••●••● 👓 ●••●••●••●••●

A guy threw a gallon of milk at my head!

How dairy!

What is Harry Potter's favorite way of getting downhill?

J.K. Rowling.

●·●··●···●··● 👓 ●··●·●··●··●··●

How does sushi like their steak cooked?

Raw.

●·●··●···●··● 👓 ●··●·●··●··●··●

What did the nut say when it was leaving?

"Cashew on the flip side!"

●·●··●···●··● 👓 ●··●·●··●··●··●

Nut jokes crack me up!

When does a sandwich cook?

When it's bacon lettuce and tomato!

•●•••●•••●•• ⌒⌒ ••●•••●•••●••

Have you heard of the movie "Constipation?"

"No."

Oh, that's probably because it hasn't come out yet.

•●•••●•••●•• ⌒⌒ ••●•••●•••●••

What do you call an Argentinian with a rubber toe?

Roberto!

•●•••●•••●•• ⌒⌒ ••●•••●•••●••

Why do scuba divers always fall backwards into the water?

Because if they fell forward, they'd still be in the boat!

Did you hear about the kidnapping at school?

It's fine, she woke up.

●●●●●●●●●● 👓 ●●●●●●●●●●

What's the difference between a piano, a tuna, and a bottle of glue?

You can tuna piano, but you can't piano a tuna!

What about the glue, you ask? I knew you would get stuck on that one!

●●●●●●●●●● 👓 ●●●●●●●●●●

Did you hear about the cheese factory that exploded in France?

There was nothing left but de Brie!

●●●●●●●●●● 👓 ●●●●●●●●●●

What did the pirate say on his 80th birthday?

"Aye Matey!"

I once bought shoes from a drug dealer.

I don't know what he laced them with, but I was tripping all day!

What kind of shoes do kidnappers wear?

White Vans!

Why can't you trust trees?

Because they're all shady!

Guess who I saw today...

Everyone I looked at!

What kind of boat never sinks?

A friendship!

eBay is so useless!

I used it to look up lighters and all i got was 13,749 matches!

Two strings got tangled together.

They said it was knot funny!

What do you do if you're on a remote island?

Try to find the TV island it belongs to!

What did the Pacific Ocean say when it saw the Atlantic Ocean?

Nothing. They just waved.

●·●··●···●··● 👓 ●·●··●··●··●

Did you know that protons have mass?

I didn't even know they were catholic!

●·●··●···●··● 👓 ●·●··●··●··●

What did the traffic light say to the passing car?

"Don't look at me; I'm changing!"

●·●··●···●··● 👓 ●·●··●··●··●

What do mermaids wash their fins with?

Tide.

What did the fried rice say to the shrimp?

Don't wok away from me!

••••••••••• 👓 ••••••••••••

Have you heard about the superhero who always works out?

He's Thor.

•••••••••••• 👓 ••••••••••••

Did you know, on average, people always want three covers on their bed?

That's just a blanket statement.

•••••••••••• 👓 ••••••••••••

Why are fish easy to weigh?

Because they have their own scales!

What does a clock do when it's hungry?

It goes back four seconds!

Did you know during King Arthur's time, one of the knights of the round table collected taxes?

His name was Sir Charge.

Did you know Montrell Jordan is a famous gardener now? He's got his own store and everything! Do you know the name of it?

This is how we greeeewwww it…. This is how we grew it!

How do bovines do math?

With a cow-culator!

A cop caught two kids playing with a firework and a car battery.

He charged one, and let the other one off.

What kind of shoes do gophers wear?

Wood Chucks!

Did you hear that Steve Harvey got into a fight with his wife?

It was a Family Feud!

What do you call someone who gets mad when they don't have any bread?

Lack toast intolerant!

Where can you grow a chef?

Bakersfield!

●·●··●···●··●● 👓 ●··●·●··●··●··●

What's Starbucks's favorite city?

Fort Lattedale!

●·●··●···●··●● 👓 ●··●·●··●··●··●

How do you get over your fear of elevators?

Just take steps to avoid them!

●·●··●···●··●● 👓 ●··●·●··●··●··●

Why do seagulls fly over the sea?

Because if they flew over the bay, they would be called bagels!

Where does the general keep his armies?

In his sleevies!

• • • • • • • • • • • 👓 • • • • • • • • • • •

What do you call syrup with a speech impediment?

Ms. Stuttersworth!

• • • • • • • • • • • 👓 • • • • • • • • • • •

What kind of car does an egg drive?

A Yolkswagen!

• • • • • • • • • • • 👓 • • • • • • • • • • •

Who's king of the classroom?

The ruler!

Why does a moon rock taste better than an Earth rock?

Because it's a little meteor.

• • • • • • • • • • • 👓 • • • • • • • • • • •

My daughter's math teacher called her average.

I think she's mean.

• • • • • • • • • • • 👓 • • • • • • • • • • •

People are usually shocked when they find out I'm not a very good electrician.

• • • • • • • • • • • 👓 • • • • • • • • • • •

What did the plumber say to the singer?

"Nice pipes!"

I don't always roll a joint...

But when I do, it's usually an ankle.

Where is the most crunk place to go to the bathroom?

The Lil' Jon!

How do you make a tissue dance?

Put a little boogie in it!

Why couldn't the angle get a loan?

His parent's wouldn't cosine!

Do you know why Waldo is always wearing a striped shirt?

He doesn't want to be spotted!

• • • • • • • • • • •  • • • • • • • • • • •

Have you heard about this new high-tech broom that's sweeping the nation?

• • • • • • • • • • •  • • • • • • • • • • •

Where do math teachers like to vacation?

At Times Square!

• •

What did the vinaigrette say to the refrigerator?

"Shut the door, I'm dressing!"

Why is it hard for lifeguards to save hippies?

Because they are too far out!

Did you hear about the new anti gravity book?

I heard once you start reading it, you can't put it down!

What kind of nails do carpenters hate to hammer?

Fingernails!

What kind of tree do math teachers climb?

Geometry!

How do robots eat guacamole?

With computer chips!

• • • • • • • • • • 👓 • • • • • • • • • •

Nut jokes are not all they're cracked up to be.

• • • • • • • • • • 👓 • • • • • • • • • •

Why is it okay for an ice company to commit fraud?

Their assets are already frozen!

• • • • • • • • • • 👓 • • • • • • • • • •

What is a pig's favorite karate move?

The pork chop!

Bought my friend a new refrigerator for her birthday.

I can't wait to see her face light up when she opens it!

6:30 is the best time on the clock; hands down!

Why are archeologists always annoyed?

Because they have a bone to pick!

How do you know when the moon is totally broke?

When it's down to it's last quarter!

How do you handle a redhead's temper?

Gingerly.

• • • • • • • • • • • 👓 • • • • • • • • • • •

I just realized my countertop is made of marble.

I've been taking it for granite all these years!

• • • • • • • • • • • 👓 • • • • • • • • • • •

If you eat alphabet soup, chances are you're going to have a vowel movement!

• • • • • • • • • • • 👓 • • • • • • • • • • •

What's Dr. Pepper's occupation?

He's a fizzicist!

What are the strongest days of the week?

Saturdays and Sundays! All other days are weak days!

●·●··●··●·●··● 👓 ●·●··●··●·●··●

What is the last part of the body to stop working?

Pupils, because they dilate!

●·●··●··●·●··● 👓 ●·●··●··●·●··●

Want to buy a broken barometer?

No pressure.

●·●··●··●·●··● 👓 ●·●··●··●·●··●

I have a pen that can write underwater.

It can also write other words.

It's important to keep candy in your pocket at all times.

It could be a lifesaver!

What's the best kind of pizza?

Plain. Nothing tops it!

Why is it good luck to say "break-a-leg" to an actor?

Because every play needs a cast!

What did Rafiki say to Simba when he was walking too slow?

Mufasa!

A Hyundai Sonata is just a Korean classical music car.

●·•··•···•·•• 👓 ●··•·•··•···•·••

Saw an Apple store get robbed today!

Does that make me an iWitness?

●·•··•···•·•• 👓 ●··•·•··•···•·••

What do you call fake potatoes?

Imitaters!

●·•··•···•·•• 👓 ●··•·•··•···•·••

What do you call a monkey in a minefield?

Baboom!

Why do basic girls travel in odd numbers?

Because they can't even!

Slept like a log last night.

Woke up in the fireplace.

What was the slogan at the shoe repair shop?

"I'll heel you. I'll save your sole. I'll even dye for you!"

I just saw a friend of mine sweep a girl off her feet!

He's quite the aggressive janitor.

You've heard of Murphy's Law, but have you heard of Cole's Law?

It's finely chopped cabbage.

•••••••••• 👓 •••••••••••

Why didn't the toilet paper cross the road?

Because it got stuck in a crack!

•••••••••• 👓 •••••••••••

True fact:

Before the crowbar was invented, most crows drank at home.

•••••••••• 👓 •••••••••••

The other day my vacuum cleaner died.

I guess you can say it bit the dust!

What's E.T. short for?

Because he's got little legs!

What's the difference between a hippo and a zippo?

Ones a little heavy, and the other is a little lighter!

Why did the can crusher quit his job?

Because it was soda pressing.

●·●···●··●··●● 👓 ●●··●··●···●·●●

What kind of bird always forgets the words to songs?

A hummingbird!

How do mountains see?

They peak!

••••••••••• 👓 ••••••••••

Never take advice from electrons.

It's always negative.

••••••••••• 👓 ••••••••••

There are no Absolut's in life.

Only vodka.

••••••••••• 👓 ••••••••••

I am an anti social vegan.

I avoid meet.

How many apples grow on a tree?

All of them!

•·•··•··•·••  ••·•··•··•··••

"Hey man, do you want this pamphlet?"

"Brochure!"

•·•··•··•·••  ••·•··•··•··••

What do you call a priest who becomes a lawyer?

A Father-in-law!

•·•··•··•·•• 👓 ••·•··•··•··••

Why didn't the coffee pot have any coffee?

Because he was mugged!

How do you find Will Smith in the snow?

You look for fresh prints!

How did the geologist student drown?

His grades were below sea level.

What creature is smarter than a talking parrot?

A spelling bee!

I have a pet tree.

It's kind of like having a pet dog, but the bark is a whole lot quieter!

I have two watchdogs.

Their names are Rolex and Timex.

I can't take my dog to the park anymore because the ducks keep attacking him!

I guess that's what I get for owning a pure-bread dog.

What kind of dog doesn't bark?

A hush puppy!

What do a dog and a cell phone have in common?

They both have collar ID!

What did the baby corn say to the momma corn?

Where's pop corn?

●•●··•●··•●··•●  ●•●··•●··•●··•●

What were the peanut's famous last words?

"Be back in a JIF!"

●•●··•●··•●··•●  ●•●··•●··•●··•●

Here's a fun fact for you. 70% of the Earth is made up of water and virtually none of it is carbonated.

So this means, the Earth, in fact, is flat.

●•●··•●··•●··•●  ●•●··•●··•●··•●

Want to know my secret for always staying down to Earth?

Gravity!

Why can't a bicycle stand on it's own?

Because it's two tired!

●·●··●···●··●·· 👓 ●··●···●··●··●

Why can't you hear a Pterodactyl use the restroom?

Because the P is silent!

●·●··●···●··●·· 👓 ●··●···●··●··●

A slice of apple pie is $2.50 in Jamaica and $3.00 in the Bahamas.

These are the pie rates of the Caribbean.

●·●··●···●··●·· 👓 ●··●···●··●··●

Grocery store checker, "paper or plastic?"

Mom, "Either. I'm bisacktual!"

What do vegetarian zombies like to eat?

Grains!

•••••••••••• 👓 ••••••••••••

My sister bet me $15 I couldn't build a car out of spaghetti.

You should have seen her face as I drove pasta!

•••••••••••• 👓 ••••••••••••

No matter how much you push the envelope, it will always be stationery!

•••••••••••• 👓 ••••••••••••

What did one plate say to the other plate?

"Lunch is on me!"

What's the best way to communicate with someone in prison?

On a cell phone!

I cut down a tree using only my vision!

It's true! I saw it with my own eyes!

What kind of car does a snake drive?

An ana-honda.

I just read a few facts about frogs.

They were ribbiting!

What do you call a deer with no eyes?

No i-deer!

• • • • • • • • • • 👓 • • • • • • • • • • •

What do you call a deer with no eyes and no legs?

Still no i-deer!

• • • • • • • • • • 👓 • • • • • • • • • • •

My friend couldn't afford to pay his water bill...

So I sent him a "get well soon" card.

• • • • • • • • • • 👓 • • • • • • • • • • •

The work week is so rough that after Monday and Tuesday, even the calendar says W.T.F!

How can you tell all ants are girls?

Well, if they were boys, they'd be called uncles.

Last night a friend and I watched three movies back to back!

Unfortunately, I was the one facing away from the TV.

What do you get when you wrap a baby owl in a wet rag?

A moist owlette!

• • • • • • • • • • • • 👓 • • • • • • • • • • • •

Want to hear a joke about a piece of paper?

Nevermind, it's tearable!

What's the leading cause of dry skin?

Towels.

•••••••••••• 👓 ••••••••••••

Two wind turbines are in a field. One turns to the other and says, "What's your favorite music?"

The other replies, "I'm a big metal fan!"

•••••••••••• 👓 ••••••••••••

A pun walks into a bar and kills ten people.

Pun in, ten dead.

•••••••••••• 👓 ••••••••••••

A lot of people don't believe in global warming.

It would be a lot cooler if they did.

What two words will open many doors for you in life?

Push and pull.

What happened to the person who stole a calendar on New Year's eve?

He got 12 months!

What kind of shoes does a thief wear?

Sneakers!

What do you call a knight who is afraid to fight?

Sir Render!

How does a penguin build its house?

Igloos it together!

• • • • • • • • • • 👓 • • • • • • • • • • •

Why did the Queen go to the dentist?

To get her tooth crowned!

• • • • • • • • • • 👓 • • • • • • • • • • •

How do you get a farm girl to like you?

A tractor!

• • • • • • • • • • 👓 • • • • • • • • • • •

Why was the hurricane so suspicious?

It caught wind of something!

How much room do fungi need to grow?

As mushroom as possible!

•••••••••••• 👓 ••••••••••••

What did the daddy spider say to the baby spider?

You spend way too much time on the web!

•••••••••••• 👓 ••••••••••••

What building has the most stories?

A library!

•••••••••••• 👓 ••••••••••••

What did the duck say to the pharmacist?

"Give me some Chapstick and put it on my bill!"

How much does a hipster weigh?

An Instagram!

•·•··•··•·••  •··•··•·•·••

I'm opening a store called moderation.

It will have everything in it!

•·•··•··•·••  •··•··•·•·••

As a lumberjack, I know that I've cut down exactly 2,417 trees.

I know because each time I cut one, I keep a log.

•·•··•··•·•• 👓 •··•··•·•·••

I asked my husband if he would like to join me for yoga.

He replied, "Namaste right here."

I once took a photo of a wheat field.

It turned out very grainy.

• • • • • • • • • • 👓 • • • • • • • • • •

Someone stole my toilet...

Police say they have nothing to go on.

• • • • • • • • • • 👓 • • • • • • • • • •

Be kind to your dentist.

He has fillings too.

• • • • • • • • • • 👓 • • • • • • • • • •

Did you know you can't breathe through your nose while smiling?

Haha! Made you smile!

Why is the sea so salty?

Because the land never waves back!

• • • • • • • • • 👓 • • • • • • • • •

What color is the wind?

Blew.

• • • • • • • • • 👓 • • • • • • • • •

Did you know that Darth Vader has a sister?

Her name is Ella. Ella Vader.

• • • • • • • • • 👓 • • • • • • • • •

I had this crazy dream where I was virtually weightless...

I was like O-MG!

What do you call a hen that counts her eggs?

A mathememachicken!

• • • • • • • • • 👓 • • • • • • • • • •

Why shouldn't you marry a tennis player?

Because "love" means nothing to them.

• • • • • • • • • 👓 • • • • • • • • • •

What did the grape say when it got stepped on?

Nothing. It just let out a little wine.

• • • • • • • • • 👓 • • • • • • • • • •

How do you put a baby alien to sleep?

You rocket!

I'm looking to sell my Delorean.

Good shape, low mileage, only driven from time to time.

●·●··●··●·●··● 👓 ●··●··●··●·●··●

How do you destroy a shopping center?

You de-mall-ish it!

●·●··●··●·●··● 👓 ●··●··●··●·●··●

How much does a Chinese dumpling weigh?

Wonton!

●·●··●··●·●··● 👓 ●··●··●··●·●··●

What does a house wear?

Address!

What do you call friends you like to eat with?

Tastebuds!

──────── 👓 ────────

What is the meaning of "opaque?"

I'm not sure. It's unclear.

──────── 👓 ────────

Apparently you can't use beefstew as a password.

It's not stroganoff!

──────── 👓 ────────

What do you call a sad cup of coffee?

Depresso!

My friend Jack claims he can talk to vegetables.

Jack and the beans talk!

•·•··•··•·•• 👓 •·•·••·•··•··•

My friends tell me I'm emotionless.

I'm not sure how I feel about it.

That's a nice ham you have there.

Be a shame if someone put a "s" in front of it and an "e" behind it.

What do you call a number that can't sit still?

A romin' numeral!

Why do chicken coops have only two doors?

Because if they had four, they'd be chicken sedans!

• • • • • • • • • • • • 👓 • • • • • • • • • • • •

What do you call a factory that sells passable products?

A satisfactory.

• • • • • • • • • • • • 👓 • • • • • • • • • • • •

Why do people in Athens hate getting up early?

Because Dawn is tough on Greece!

• • • • • • • • • • • • 👓 • • • • • • • • • • • •

What's the definition of a will?

It's a dead giveaway!

Moms in the year 2020:

"I'll have a Corona, hold the virus!"

•·•··•··•··•• 👓 ••·•··•··•··••

Did you know if you boil a funny bone it becomes a laughing stock?

That's humerus!

•·•··•··•··•• 👓 ••·•··•··•··••

Five out of six doctors believe that Russian Roulette isn't harmful.

•·•··•··•··•• 👓 ••·•··•··•··••

Have you heard of the band 123MB?

They haven't gotten a gig yet!

If you lose your hearing, is it ear replaceable?

England doesn't have a kidney bank...

But it does have a Liverpool!

What to hear a leech joke?

Nevermind, it really sucks!

What are the only acceptable jokes to tell during a quarantine?

Inside jokes.

What do you call a man that can't stand?

Neil.

•·•··•···•··•• 👓 •··•··•···•··•

Why do people in Antarctica seem to never catch viruses?

Because they are ice-o-lated!

•·•··•···•··•• 👓 •··•··•···•··•

No matter how many times I tried to uninstall and reinstall 2020, it always had a nasty virus!

•·•··•···•··•• 👓 •··•··•···•··•

Who is the social distancing champion?

Bigfoot!

Why were Native American's popular in the year 2020?

Because they had all the TP's!

• • • • • • • • • • • 👓 • • • • • • • • • • •

The amount of jokes surrounding the year 2020 is starting to reach worrying numbers.

Some scientists claim it may be remembered as a pundemic!

• • • • • • • • • • • 👓 • • • • • • • • • • •

What happens if you're stuck in quarantine for too long?

You become a quaran-adult!

• • • • • • • • • • • 👓 • • • • • • • • • • •

I tried to come up with some good jokes about social distancing...

But this is as close as I could get.

What kind of magic do cows believe in?

Moodoo!

••••••••••  ••••••••••

Today, my boss told us the employee with the worst posture will be fired!

I have a hunch, it will be me.

••••••••••  ••••••••••

The word "diputseromneve" may look ridiculous...

But backwards it's "even more stupid!"

••••••••••  ••••••••••

Organic Chemistry is difficult.

Those who study it have alkynes of trouble!

What do you call a laughing motorcycle?

A Yamahahaha!

What do you say to a Mexican body builder who just ran out of protein?

"No whey, Jose!"

I asked my friend Sam to sing a song about the iPhone.

And then, Samsung.

Why is bread like the sun?

It rises in the yeast and sets in the waist!

Why are chemists bad at playing pranks?

They lack the element of surprise!

• • • • • • • • • • •  • • • • • • • • • • •

The machine at the coin factory just stopped working!

It doesn't make any sense!

• • • • • • • • • • •  • • • • • • • • • • •

Yes, English can be weird.

It can be understood through tough thorough thought, though.

• •

Why was Cinderella thrown off the baseball team?

Because she ran away from the ball!

Why did the pig decide to pursue a career making bread?

Because he was good at bacon!

What do you call people who take care of chickens?

Chicken Tenders!

How do you make a water bed more bouncy?

You put spring water in it!

•·•··•···•··• 👓 •··•··•···•··•

What happens when you smack Dwayne Johnson's butt?

You hit rock bottom!

What's the difference between Dubai and Abu Dhabi?

The people in Dubai don't like the Flintstones. But the people in Abu Dhabi do!

Why was the math book so sad?

Because it had so many problems!

My grandfather is 85 and doesn't need glasses!

He drinks straight from the bottle!

I hired a handyman yesterday and gave him a list of six things to do.

He only did numbers 1, 3, & 5 on the list. Turns out he only does odd jobs.

Did you know Stephen King has a son named Joe?

I'm not joking, but he is!

Did you hear about the new restaurant on the moon?

Great food, no atmosphere!

Why did the cookie cry?

Because his father was a wafer so long!

Why can't dyslexic people tell jokes?

They always punch up the mess line!

I told my sister I think she's drawing her eyebrows on too high.

She looked surprised.

Where do you learn to make ice cream?

In sundae school!

Went to a Mexican restaurant.

The waitress didn't talk much, but after some stumbling, she sure did spill the beans!

There is a new deodorant on the market called "Ventriloquist!"

It doesn't do anything about your body odor, but people will think it's coming from the person next to you.

Why was the guy who stole a hay stack in jail?

Because he couldn't make bale.

How do construction workers party?

They raise the roof!

A pirate walks into a bar with a paper towel on his head! Bartender says, "Hey buddy, what's up with the paper towel on your head?"

Pirate says, "Aaarrrggg, I've got a Bounty on me head!"

What kind of guns do bees use?

BB guns!

Did you know there's no official training for a trash collector?

They just pick it up as they go!

•·•··•··•··• 👓 •·•··•··•··•

How did the frog burn his mouth?

He tried to eat a Firefly!

•·•··•··•··• 👓 •·•··•··•··•

What is Whitney Houston's favorite type of coordination?

Haaannnddd eeeyyyyyeeee!

•·•··•··•··• 👓 •·•··•··•··•

What does a baker do when he's happy?

Abundance!

It's easy to convince ladies not to eat Tide Pods.

But it's a lot harder to deter gents!

Why was the weightlifter upset?

She works with dumbbells!

Why did the square triangle go to the gym?

To get back into shape!

Why was the sand wet?

Because the sea weed!

Why should you always knock on your fridge before opening it?

In case there's a salad dressing!

My boss said, "You are the worse train operator ever! How many trains have you derailed in the last year?"

I said, "I'm not sure, it's hard to keep track!"

Did you hear about the guy who's left side got cut off in a horrible accident?

He's all right now.

Why did the Invisible Man turn down the job offer?

He couldn't see himself doing it.

My son's class is taking a trip to the Coca-Cola factory.

I told him to pay attention in case there's a pop quiz!

My wife is on a tropical food diet; the house is full of this stuff!

It's enough to make a mango crazy!

I hate how funerals are always at 9am.

I'm not really a mourning person.

What do you get when you cross a chicken with a bell?

An alarm cluck!

When you take apart and clean out a vacuum cleaner, does that make you a vacuum cleaner?

I just read a book about Stockholm Syndrome.

It was really bad at first, but by the end, I liked it.

A termite walks into a bar and says...

"Is the bar tender here?"

A sandwich walks into a bar.

Bartender says, "sorry mate, we don't serve food in here!"

A man got hit in the head by a can of Coke!

He's okay, but only because it was a soft drink.

•·•··•···•··• 👓 •·•··•···•··•

What day do chickens dislike the most?

Fry-days!

•·•··•···•··• 👓 •·•··•···•··•

Want to hear a joke about pizza?

Nevermind, it's cheesy!

•·•··•···•··• 👓 •·•··•···•··•

How did the chicken cross the road?

In a carry-out bag!

Gravity is one of the most fundamental forces of the Universe! What do you get when you remove it?

Gravy.

●・●・・・●・・●・・●● 👓 ●●・●・・●・・●・●・●

Yesterday I spotted an albino Dalmatian.

It was the least I could do for him.

●・●・・●・・・●・・●● 👓 ●●・●・・●・・●・●・●

How is a golf ball different from a Ford?

You can drive a golf ball 200 yds!

●・●・・●・・・●・・●● 👓 ●●・●・・●・●・●・●

Within a matter of minutes, the detective discovered what the murder weapon was.

It was a brief case.

Why do nurses like red crayons?

Because sometimes they have to draw blood.

• • • • • • • • • • 👓 • • • • • • • • • • •

Why should you never have a staring contest with your male offspring?

Because the son always wins!

• • • • • • • • • • 👓 • • • • • • • • • • •

What did the janitor say when he jumped out of the closet?

"Supplies!"

• • • • • • • • • • 👓 • • • • • • • • • • •

The Lego stores have reopened!

People are lined up for blocks!

What do you call an annoyed lobster?

A crustration.

•··•···•···•··• 👓 •··•···•··•··••

Where do you take someone who has been injured in a peek-a-boo accident?

To the I.C.U.!

•··•···•···•··• 👓 •··•···•··•··••

What do you get when you mix prune juice with holy water?

A religious movement!

•··•···•···•··• 👓 •··•···•··•··••

Why is diarrhea hereditary?

Because it runs down your genes!

I love jokes about eyes.

The cornea, the better!

•·•··•··•·•• 👓 •··•··•··•··••

What's the best way to quit being vegan?

Cold turkey!

•·•··•··•·•• 👓 •··•··•··•··••

What did Forrest Gump say in the Italian restaurant?

"I love you penne!"

•·•··•··•·•• 👓 •··•··•··•··••

What do you call karate for amputees?

Partial art!

Why should you never drink 8 Coca-colas?

You might throw 7-up!

• • • • • • • • • •  • • • • • • • • • • •

What has four wheels and flies?

A garbage truck!

• • • • • • • • • •  • • • • • • • • • • •

What type of tree fits in your hand?

A palm tree!

• • • • • • • • • • 👓 • • • • • • • • • • •

Never attack people with stringed instruments!

Violins is not the answer!

Who can drink two liters of gasoline?

Jerry can!

••••••••••• 👓 •••••••••••

What did 50 Cent do when he was hungry?

58!

••••••••••• 👓 •••••••••••

Last night I ate seafood for dinner.

Today I'm feeling rather eel...

••••••••••• 👓 •••••••••••

Sundays are a little sad.

But the day before is a sadder day.

What is the meteorologists favorite piece of jewelry?

A tornado watch!

••••••••••• 👓 ••••••••••••

Why is Pavlov's hair so soft?

He conditioned it!

••••••••••• 👓 ••••••••••••

Who do mice pray to?

Cheeseus!

••••••••••• 👓 ••••••••••••

What currency do astronauts use in space?

Starbucks!

What happens if you don't pay your exorcist?

You get repossessed!

• • • • • • • • • • • 👓 • • • • • • • • • • •

Turquoise is the best color?

It's CYANtifically proven!

• • • • • • • • • • • 👓 • • • • • • • • • • •

What do hockey players and magicians have in common?

Hat tricks!

• • • • • • • • • • • 👓 • • • • • • • • • • •

What kind of exercise do lazy people do?

Diddly squats!

How do you say "sup dawg" in Chinese?

Konichihuahua!

• • • • • • • • • • 👓 • • • • • • • • • • •

What kind of hair does the ocean have?

Wavy!

• • • • • • • • • • 👓 • • • • • • • • • • •

What's a highlighter's favorite Twister position?

Knee on yellow!

• • • • • • • • • • 👓 • • • • • • • • • • •

How do scientist keep their breath fresh?

Experimints!

Where do movie previews live?

At the trailer park!

• • • • • • • • • • • 👓 • • • • • • • • • • •

Which superhero hits the most homeruns?

Batman!

• • • • • • • • • • • 👓 • • • • • • • • • • •

What's Batman's favorite fruit?

Banananananananana... Grapefruit!

• • • • • • • • • • • 👓 • • • • • • • • • • •

My helium balloon business is reaching new heights!

My customers speak highly of it!

What kind of music are balloons afraid of?

Pop music!

•··•···•···•··•• 👓 ••·•···•··•···••

Why did the baker's wife divorce him?

He was too kneady!

•··•···•···•··•• 👓 ••·•···•··•···••

If you cross your fingers after surgery, you'll heal faster!

Or maybe that's just super stitchin'.

•··•···•···•··•• 👓 ••·•···•··•···••

What do you call it when pilots get influenza?

The flew!

Why it it a good idea to buy shares when you're feeling lonely?

So you have some company!

•·•··•···•··• 👓 •··•··•··•··•

If you catch the Corona twice, it will now be called Dos Equis.

I'm really proud of my nose!

I picked it myself.

Police arrested the world tongue-twister champion.

They said he will be given a tough sentence.

If male birth control isn't called "son block,"
we have failed as a society.

• • • • • • • • • 👓 • • • • • • • • • •

I was recently let go from my job as a
lumberjack.

Apparently I had too many axe-idents.

• • • • • • • • • 👓 • • • • • • • • • •

Do backwards poets write inverse?

• • • • • • • • • 👓 • • • • • • • • • •

Someone asked if I was athletic.

I said, "why of course I am! I surf the
internet every day!"

If Satan ever lost his hair, there would be hell toupee!

••••••••••• 👓 ••••••••••

S.P.A.M.

Stuff posing as meat.

What do you call someone who steals bananas?

A bananadit!

As I get older, I think about all the people I've lost over the years.

Maybe "Trail Guide" wasn't the best career choice.

You really got to hand it to short people.

They usually can't reach it anyways.

••••••••••• 👓 •••••••••••

A Spanish magician told the audience he would disappear on the count of three. He said, "Uno, dos..."

poof

He disappeared without a tres!

•••••••••••• 👓 •••••••••••

An invisible man marries an invisible woman.

Their kids weren't much to look at either.

•••••••••••• 👓 •••••••••••

What happens when the King leaves the toilet?

A royal flush!

Who was the Roman empire who never aged past nineteen?

Constantine!

My daughter asked what it was like to be a parent.

That night, I woke her up at 2:00 am and told her I lost my sock.

Just bought a new camera, but I'm going to return it because it's unpredictable.

It's a loose Cannon.

Someone tried to sell me a coffin today.

That's the last thing I need.

What did the fish say to the beaver?

"Excuse me sir, you've clogged my toilet!"

•·•··•···•··••  •·•··•···•··•••

I'm reading a horror book in braille.

Something bad is going to happen soon... I can feel it.

•·•··•···•··••  •·•··•···•··•••

My doctor told me to drink two glasses of wine after a hot bath...

I didn't drink the wine because I couldn't even finish the bath!

•·•··•···•··••  •·•··•···•··•••

My doctor told me I suffer from paranoia.

Well, he didn't say it in those words, but I could tell that's what he was thinking!

I once ate a kid's meal at McDonald's.

The mom got really angry.

•••••••••••• 👓 ••••••••••••

I wanted to marry my English teacher when he got out of jail.

But apparently you can't end a sentence with a proposition.

•••••••••••• 👓 ••••••••••••

What's the longest word in the English language?

"Smiles"

The first and last letter are a mile apart!

•••••••••••• 👓 ••••••••••••

Did you know to start a zoo you need two pandas, a grizzly, and a polar bear.

It's the bear minimum.

I was driving my car when pirates jumped in and stole everything!

They were pirates of the car-I-be-in.

•·•··•·•··•• 👓 ••·•··•···•··•

What's a DJ's favorite sauce?

Marinara... mar-i-nar-a.

•·•··•·•··•• 👓 ••·•··•···•··•

I read a law that said you're supposed to turn on your headlights when it's raining in Sweden.

How am I supposed to know when it's raining in Sweden?

•·•··•·•··•• 👓 ••·•··•···•··•

If lightning strikes an orchestra, who is most likely to get hit?

The conductor!

I spilled spot remover on my dog.

Doggone.

I sympathize with batteries...

I'm not included in anything either.

A guy new to the gym asked his trainer what machine to use to get beautiful girls.

The trainer told him to use the ATM outside.

•·•··•··•··• 👓 •··•··•··•·•

When I started dating my husband, he used to go on and on about bees.

I guess that's when I knew... he was a keeper.

A fisherman started dating a mermaid.

They met online.

• • • • • • • • • •  • • • • • • • • • • •

I am not one to usually brag about my finances...

But my credit card company just called to tell me that my balance is outstanding!

• • • • • • • • • •  • • • • • • • • • • •

Getting my drone stuck in a tree isn't the worse thing that has happened to me today.

It's definitely up there!

• • • • • • • • • • 👓 • • • • • • • • • • •

I threw a ball for my dog.

A little extravagant, I know. But he looks amazing in a tuxedo!

How do you milk sheep?

With iPhone accessories!

• • • • • • • • • • 👓 • • • • • • • • • •

I got mugged by six dwarfs last night.

Not happy.

• • • • • • • • • • 👓 • • • • • • • • • •

What's a ten letter word that starts with gas?

Pooooooop!

• • • • • • • • • • 👓 • • • • • • • • • •

I'm writing a book about reverse psychology.

Do not read it!

I just finished reading a book about teleportation.

It took me to so many places!

••••••••••••• 👓 ••••••••••••••

I used to play piano by ear.

Now, I use my hands.

•••••••••••••• 👓 ••••••••••••••

What's halfway between a small night and a large night?

Midnight.

•••••••••••••• 👓 ••••••••••••••

What can you find in the middle of nowhere?

The letter "H!"

VALENTINE'S DAY

What did Robinhood say to his girlfriend?

"Sherwood like to be your valentine!"

•··•··•··•··•··• 👓 •··•··•··•··•··•

What do you call two birds in love?

Tweet-hearts!

•··•··•··•··•··• 👓 •··•··•··•··•··•

What did one boat say to another?

"Are you up for a little rowmance?"

•··•··•··•··•··• 👓 •··•··•··•··•··•

My husband asked if we have a date for Valentine's Day.

I said, "yes, it's February 14th."

My new boyfriend works at the zoo.

I think he's a keeper.

Did you hear about the near-sighted porcupine?

He fell in love with a pincushion!

Why was the woman so hungry for love?

Because she had no idea where her next male was coming from!

What did the patient with the broken leg say to the doctor?

"Hey doc, I have a crutch on you!"

If I ever need a heart transplant, I want my ex's.

It has never been used.

You shouldn't laugh at your boyfriend's choices.

You're one of them!

Love is like a fart.

If you force it, you're going to make a mess!

·•·•·•··•·•··•• 👓 ••·•··•·••·•·••

What did one coffee bean say to the other on Valentine's day?

"You mocha me happy!"

What do you call a group of musical whales who serenade their Valentine?

An orca-stra!

Why did the smartphone break up with the charger on Valentine's Day?

It was tired of being in a committed relationship.

What did the calculator say to its Valentine?

"You can count on me!"

What did one pickle say to the other on Valentine's Day?

"You mean a great dill to me!"

Why did the boy bring a ladder to his girlfriend's house on Valentine's Day?

He wanted to take their relationship to the next level!

What did one magnet say to another on Valentine's Day?

"I find you very attractive!"

What did the stamp say to the envelope on Valentine's Day?

"Stick with me and we'll go places!"

What did one light bulb say to the other on Valentine's Day?

"I love you a watt!"

What did the boy octopus say to the girl octopus on Valentine's Day?

"I want to hold your hand, hand, hand, hand, hand, hand, hand, hand."

What's the best part about Valentine's Day?

The day after when all the chocolate is on sale!

What did one volcano say to the other on Valentine's Day?

"I lava you!"

How did the cellphone propose to its charger?

It gave it a ring!

ST. PATRICK'S DAY

What country has the fastest growing population?

Ireland. Every day it's Dublin!

What do you call a bulletproof Irishman?

Rick O-shea!

Why is running with bagpipes a bad idea?

You could put an aye out, or better yet, get kilt!

What's Irish and stays outside all year long?

Paddy-O Furniture!

What do you call a fake Irish stone?

A sham-rock!

How can you spot a jealous shamrock?

It's always green with envy!

What do you call a big Irish spider?

Paddy long legs!

Why shouldn't you iron a four-leaf clover?

Because you'll press your luck!

What do you call a polite leprechaun?

A little "charm"-ing!

Why do leprechauns make great secretaries?

Because they're really good at hiding pots of gold!

What do you get when you cross a four-leaf clover with poison ivy?

A rash of good luck!

What do you call a leprechaun who gets sent to jail?

A "lepre-con!"

Why do leprechauns love to play hide-n-seek?

Because good luck is hard to find!

What band should you listen to on St. Patrick's Day?

Green Day!

What do you call a Dwayne Johnson impersonator?

A sham-rock!

Did you know the Irish lead the World in recycling?

They like to go green!

What do you call Irish handcuffs?

A drink in both hands!

• • • • • • • • •  • • • • • • • • •

An Irish guy walks out of a bar…

No, really! It can happen!

• • • • • • • • • • • • • • • • • •

Would you like to know everything I know about leprechauns?

It's very little.

• • • • • • • • •  • • • • • • • • •

I'm really sick of all the Irish stereotypes…

As soon as I finish this drink, I'm going to go punch someone!

Irish puns on St. Patrick's Day don't just shame you...

They Shamus all!

••••••••••  ••••••••••

What is a leprechaun's favorite kind of music?

Shamrock and roll!

••••••••••  ••••••••••

Why did Saint Patrick drive all the snakes out of Ireland?

Because he couldn't afford plane fare!

•••••••••• 👓 ••••••••••

Why do people wear shamrocks on St. Patrick's Day?

Because regular rocks are too heavy!

EASTER

Why did the Easter egg hide?

Because it was a little chicken!

• • • • • • • • • • • •  • • • • • • • • • • • •

Where does the Easter Bunny get his eggs from?

An eggplant!

• • • • • • • • • • • •  • • • • • • • • • • • •

What did the Easter Bunny say to the carrot?

It has been nice gnawing on you!

• • • • • • • • • • • • 👓 • • • • • • • • • • • •

How can you tell where the Easter Bunny has been?

Eggs mark the spot!

How does a rabbit make gold soup?

He begins with 24 carrots!

•·•··•··•··•• 👓 ••·•··•··•··••

What kind of bunny can't hop?

A chocolate one!

What kind of stories are the Easter Bunny's favorite?

The kind with hoppy endings!

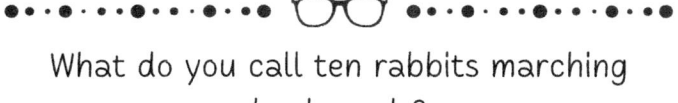

What do you call ten rabbits marching backwards?

A receding hare line!

Why shouldn't you tell an Easter egg joke?

It might crack up!

•···•··•···•·•• ⊙⊙ ••·•···•···•··•

How does the Easter Bunny stay fit?

Eggs-ercise! Specifically, Hare-obics!

•···•··•···•·•• ⊙⊙ ••·•···•···•··•

What do you call a rabbit with fleas?

Bugs Bunny!

•···•··•···•·•• ⊙⊙ ••·•···•···•··•

What did one Easter egg say to another?

"Heard any good yolks lately?"

What's the Easter Bunny's favorite type of music?

Hip-hop!

How does the Easter Bunny keep his fur looking good?

Hare spray!

What do you get when you cross a bunny with an onion?

A bunion!

Why did the Easter Bunny go to school?

To get a little egg-ucation!

DERBY INSPIRED

What kind of food does a racehorse eat?

Fast food!

•••••••••• 👓 ••••••••••

What do you call a pony with a cough?

A little horse!

•••••••••• 👓 ••••••••••

What do you call a horse who lives next door?

A neigh-bor!

•••••••••• 👓 ••••••••••

What is a horse's favorite sport?

Stable-tennis!

How does a horse from Kentucky greet another horse?

With southern horsepitality!

What did the bra say to the Derby hat?

"You go on ahead! We'll give these two a lift!"

Why are racehorses in such good shape?

They're on a strict, stable diet!

Why don't racehorses wear underwear?

It rides up on them!

What kind of bread does a racehorse eat?

Thoroughbred!

• • • • • • • • • •  • • • • • • • • • •

Where do racehorses shop?

Old Neigh-vy!

• • • • • • • • • •  • • • • • • • • • •

What do you call a well-balanced race horse?

Stable.

• • • • • • • • • • 👓 • • • • • • • • • •

Why do racehorses fart when they buck?

Because they cannot achieve full horsepower without gas!

What did the horse say when he fell down?

"Help! I've fallen, and I can't giddyup!"

• • • • • • • • • • • 👓 • • • • • • • • • • •

How do you lead a horse to water?

With good directions!

• • • • • • • • • • • 👓 • • • • • • • • • • •

Why don't horses use the computer?

Because they're afraid of the mouse!

• • • • • • • • • • • 👓 • • • • • • • • • • •

Why did the horse train to become a racehorse?

Because he wanted a stable career!

Who runs the city?

The mare, of course!

● · ● · · ● · · · ● · · ●● 👓 ●● · ● · · · ● · · ● · ●●

I bought a horse and named him Mayo.

Sometimes Mayo neighs.

● · ● · · ● · · · ● · · ●● 👓 ●● · ● · · · ● · · ● · ●●

What are you supposed to do when someone tells you to "hold your horses?"

You are supposed to be stable.

● · ● · · ● · · · ● · · ●● 👓 ●● · ● · · · ● · · ● · ●●

To horse or not to horse.

That is equestrian!

What do you call a scary horse?

A nightmare!

•·•··•··•·•• 👓 •·•··•··•·•·•

When do vampires like horse races?

When it's neck and neck.

A horse walks into a bar. Bartender says "Hey!"

Horse replies, "Yes please. You read my mind!"

Where do colts go when they are sick?

To the horsepital!

What do you call racing royalty?

A Triple Crown Prince!

What do jockeys drink after a race?

A furlong island tea!

Why are jockeys so skinny?

Because they only eat Seabiscuits and tea!

What did Victor Espinoza drink after winning the Belmont Stakes in 2015?

A shot of Triple Crown Royal!

U.S.A. INSPIRED

How come there aren't any knock knock jokes about America?

Because freedom rings!

•••••••••••• 👓 ••••••••••••

What genre are National Anthems?

Country.

•••••••••••• 👓 ••••••••••••

What do you get when you mix Captain America with The Hulk?

The star spangled banner!

•••••••••••• 👓 ••••••••••••

Why did the Statue of Liberty always win at hide-n-seek?

Because she was outstanding at it!

Did you hear the joke about the Liberty bell?

It cracked me up!

•·•··•··•·•• 👓 •··•·•··•··•·••

What do you call a bee that lives in America?

A "USB."

•·•··•··•·•• 👓 •··•·•··•··•·••

What dance was very popular in 1776?

Indepen-dance!

•·•··•··•·•• 👓 •··•·•··•··•·••

What did one US flag say to the other?

Nothing. It just waved!

What did the tourist say after leaving the Statue of Liberty?

"Keep in torch!"

What do you call doing 2,000 lbs of laundry?

Washing-ton!

What do you get from an Alaskan cow?

Ice Cream!

• · • · · • · · · • · · •   👓   • · · • · • · · · • · · •

What is the smartest state?

Alabama! It has four A's and one B!

What kind of tea did the American colonists thirst for?

Liberty!

What would you get if you crossed the American National Bird with Snoopy?

A bald beagle!

When did George Washington die?

Before they buried him.

●•●••●••●•● 👓 ●•●••●••●•●

Where did the pilgrims land when they came to America?

On their feet!

Why does the Mississippi River see so well?

Because it has four eyes!

⸺⸺⸺

Why is it easy to get into Florida?

Because it has many keys!

⸺⸺⸺

What happens when fog lifts in southern California?

UCLA!

⸺⸺⸺

In what US State can you find tiny drinks?

Minnesota!

Where was the Declaration of Independence signed?

At the bottom!

What rock group has four guys who don't sing?

Mount Rushmore!

What would you call the USA if everyone lived in their cars?

An incarnation!

Why can't a woman living in the US be buried in Canada?

Because she's still alive!

HALLOWEEN

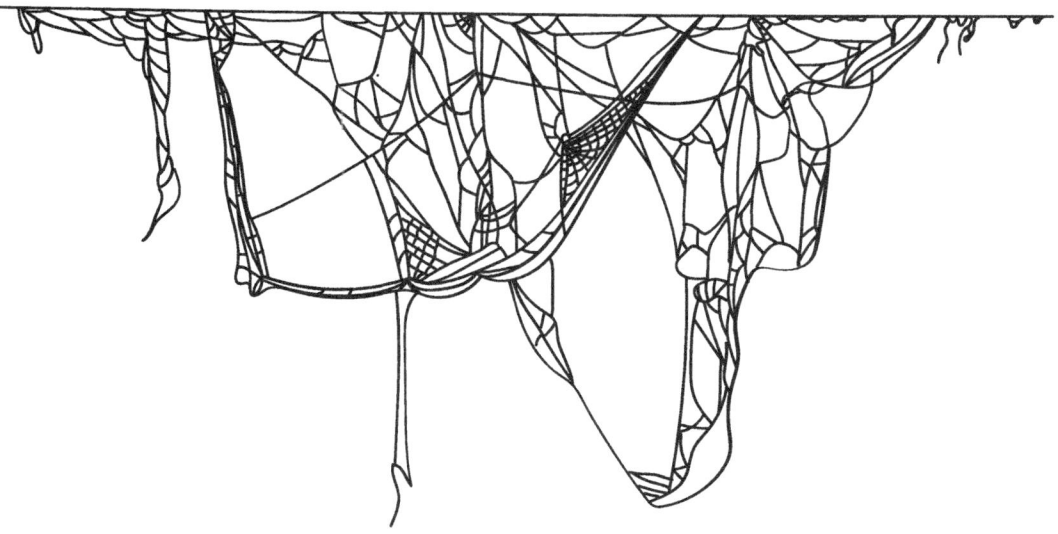

Why do demons and ghouls hang out together?

Because demons are a ghouls' best friend!

What kind of candy do eye doctors give out on Halloween?

Candy corneas!

What do Italians eat on Halloween?

Fettuccini Araid-o!

What do they teach at witching school?

Spelling!

How do you repair a broken pumpkin?

With a pumpkin patch!

Where would you imprison a skeleton?

In the rib cage!

Why did the skeleton cross the road?

To get to the body shop!

What does the baby monster call his parents?

Mummy and Deady!

Will glass coffins become popular?

Remains to be seen...

•·•··•·•··•·•• 👓 •·•··•·•··•·••

What kind of makeup do ghosts wear?

Mas-scare-a!

•·•··•·•··•·•• 👓 •·•··•·•··•·••

What do ghosts and goblins drink on Halloween?

Ghoul-aid!

•·•··•·•··•·•• 👓 •·•··•·•··•·••

What plants like Halloween the most?

Bam-boo!

What did the ghosts say to the bartender when they entered?

"We're just here for the boos!"

•••••••••••• 👓 ••••••••••••

Why do ghosts like to go out?

They love to get sheet-faced!

•••••••••••• 👓 ••••••••••••

What are a ghost's favorite kinds of streets?

A dead end.

•••••••••••• 👓 ••••••••••••

What are a ghost's second favorite kind of streets?

A boo-levard!

What do you call a goblin who gets too close to the bonfire?

Toasty ghosty!

••••••••••••• 👓 ••••••••••••••

Monsters aren't good at math...

Unless you count Dracula.

•••••••••••••• 👓 ••••••••••••••

Where do vampires keep their money?

In the blood bank!

•••••••••••••• 👓 ••••••••••••••

What's a vampire's least favorite song?

Another One Bites the Dust!

What's Dracula's favorite circus act?

He always goes for the juggler!

––––––––––––

What kind of dogs do vampires have?

A bloodhound.

––––––––––––

Why did the headless horseman start a business?

He wanted to get ahead in life!

––––––––––––

Why do ghosts make the best cheerleaders?

Because they're full of spirit!

I think the A/C unit at my work is haunted.

It keeps giving everyone the chills!

• • • • • • • • • • 👓 • • • • • • • • • •

What do you call two spiders who just got married?

Newlywebbed.

• • • • • • • • • • 👓 • • • • • • • • • •

What kind of music do mummies like listening to?

Wrap music!

• • • • • • • • • • 👓 • • • • • • • • • •

Why did the game warden arrest the ghost?

He didn't have a haunting license!

What kind of car do ghosts drive?

Boo-icks!

●·●··●·●··● 👓 ●·●··●·●··●

What's a goblin's favorite cheese?

Monster-ella!

●·●··●·●··● 👓 ●·●··●·●··●

Where do ghosts like to vacation?

Mali-boo!

●·●··●·●··● 👓 ●·●··●·●··●

Why don't ghosts have bands?

Because they're always booooooed.

Where do werewolves live?

Howllywood.

•·•··•··•·•• 👓 •··•·•··•·•••

Why didn't the vampire attack Taylor Swift?

Because she had "Bad Blood!"

•·•··•··•·•• 👓 •··•·•··•·•••

Why do they put fences around cemeteries?

Because people are dying to get in!

•·•··•··•·•• 👓 •··•·•··•·•••

What kind of Pop Tarts do ghosts like?

Boo-berry!

Why was the mummy so tense?

Because he was all wound up!

― ― ― ― ◯◯ ― ― ― ―

Why do ghosts and skeletons make bad secret agents?

Because you can see right through them!

― ― ― ― ◯◯ ― ― ― ―

Why don't mummies take vacation?

They're afraid to relax and unwind!

― ― ― ― ◯◯ ― ― ― ―

What do you call a ghost's mom and dad?

Transparents!

What do you get when you cross a snowman with a vampire?

Frostbite!

•·•··•···•··• 👓 •·•··•···•··•

Why did the skeleton go to the party alone?

Because he had no body to go with him.

•·•··•···•··• 👓 •·•··•···•··•

How do you make a witch scratch?

Take away the W!

•·•··•···•··• 👓 •·•··•···•··•

What do you call a haunted chicken?

A poultry-geist!

What do you call a monster with no neck?

The lost neck monster!

•••••••••• 👓 ••••••••••

Why did the mummy call the doctor?

Because he was in de-Nile!

•••••••••• 👓 ••••••••••

What did one pumpkin say to the other pumpkin?

"You're gourd-geous!

•••••••••• 👓 ••••••••••

What do you get when you drop a pumpkin?

Squash!

Why are skeletons always so calm?

Because nothing gets under their skin!

●·●··●··●··●·● 👓 ●·●··●··●··●·●

What kind of monster loves to disco?

The Boogieman!

●·●··●··●··●·● 👓 ●·●··●··●··●·●

What do you get when you cross a black cat with a lemon?

A sourpuss!

●·●··●··●··●·● 👓 ●·●··●··●··●·●

What is a ghost's least favorite room?

The Living Room!

THANKSGIVING

Why did the scarecrow win an award?

Because he was outstanding in his field!

●·●··●···●··●● 👓 ●·●··●···●··●●

What do you wear to Thanksgiving dinner?

A har-vest!

●·●··●···●··●● 👓 ●·●··●···●··●●

I was going to serve sweet potatoes with Thanksgiving dinner, but I accidentally sat on them.

Now, I'll be serving squash instead!

●·●··●···●··●● 👓 ●·●··●···●··●●

What kind of key has legs, but can't open a door?

A tur-key!

Why did the farmer run a steamroller over his potato field on Thanksgiving Day?

He wanted to raise mashed potatoes!

•••••••••••• 👓 ••••••••••••

What's the difference between a pirate and a cranberry farmer?

A pirate buries his treasure, but a cranberry farmer treasures his berries!

•••••••••••• 👓 ••••••••••••

What do you call a turkey on the day after Thanksgiving?

Lucky!

•••••••••••• 👓 ••••••••••••

Can a turkey jump higher than the Empire State Building?

Why yes, of course! A building can't jump!

What kind of music did the pilgrims listen to at Thanksgiving feast?

Plymouth Rock!

••••••••••••• 👓 •••••••••••••

Why did the farmer have to separate the chicken and the turkey?

He sensed fowl play!

•••••••••••••• 👓 •••••••••••••

Dad: "Honey, can you help fix Thanksgiving dinner?"

Mom: "Why? Is it broken?"

•••••••••••••• 👓 •••••••••••••

What's the most musical part of the turkey?

The drum sticks!

What did the turkey say to the hunter?

"Quack! Quack!"

••·•··•···•··•• 👓 ••·•··•···•··•••

What always smells the best at Thanksgiving?

Your nose!

••·•··•···•··•• 👓 ••·•··•···•··•••

What's a turkey's favorite dessert?

Peach gobbler!

••·•··•···•··•• 👓 ••·•··•···•··•••

Which bird is best at bowling?

A turkey!

Why did the cranberries turn red?

Because they saw the turkey dressing!

•·•··•···•·•• 👓 •·•··•·•··•·••

What sound does a limping turkey make?

Wobble, wobble.

What do you get when you cross a turkey with a centipede?

Turkey legs for everyone!

If pilgrims were alive today, what would they be known for?

Their age!

What did the turkey say to the computer?

"Google, Google, Google!"

●•●••●••●•● 👓 ●•●••●••●•●

Why do pilgrims' pants always fall?

Because they wear their buckles on their hats!

●•●••●••●•● 👓 ●•●••●••●•●

Why did the turkey sit on a tomahawk?

To hatchet a good plan for Thanksgiving!

●•●••●••●•● 👓 ●•●••●••●•●

What sound does a space turkey make?

Hubble, Hubble, Hubble!

What did one snowman say to the other?

"Do you smell carrots?"

●·●··●···●··●● 👓 ●·●··●···●··●●

Why do Dasher and Dancer love coffee?

Because they're Santa's star bucks!

●·●··●···●··●● 👓 ●·●··●···●··●●

What do you get when you cross a Christmas tree with an iPad?

A pineapple!

●·●··●···●··●● 👓 ●·●··●···●··●●

Who is a Christmas tree's favorite singer?

Spruce Springsteen!

What do reindeer say before they tell a joke?

"This will sleigh you!"

How did the Christmas ornament get addicted to Christmas?

He was hooked on trees his whole life!

What do you call an elf who sings?

A wrapper!

Why are Christmas trees so fond of the past?

Because the presents beneath them.

What's Santa's laundry detergent of choice?

Yule Tide!

●··●···●··●··●　⌒⌒　●●··●···●··●··●●

What's Santa's favorite snack food?

Crisp Pringles!

●··●···●··●··●●　⌒⌒　●●··●···●··●··●●

What does the abominable snowman do when he gets aggravated?

He takes a chill pill!

●··●···●··●··●●　⌒⌒　●●··●···●··●··●●

How do Christmas angels greet each other?

"Halo!"

Why did the snow people go to the carrot patch?

To pick their noses!

•·•··•···•··•  •··•·•··•···••

Where do Santa's elves keep their money?

In the snow bank!

•·•··•···•··•  •··•·•··•···••

How does Santa keep his bathroom immaculate?

He uses Comet!

•·•··•···•··•  •··•·•··•···••

Who is Santa's favorite singer?

Elf-is Presley!

Why doesn't Santa like it when he gets stuck in a chimney?

He gets Claus-trophobic!

•·•··•··•··•·••  •·•··•··•·•··•·••

Did Rudolph go to reindeer school?

No, he was elf-taught!

•·•··•··•··•·••  •·•··•··•·•··•·••

What kind of motorcycle does Santa ride?

Holly Davidson!

•·•··•··•··•·••  •·•··•··•·•··•·••

What always falls in the North Pole, but never gets hurt?

Snow!

What's in December that isn't in any other month?

The letter D!

• • • • • • • • • • • • 👓 • • • • • • • • • • • •

What would a reindeer do if it lost its tail?

It goes to a retail shop for a new one!

• • • • • • • • • • • • 👓 • • • • • • • • • • • •

Did you hear Santa knows karate?

He has a black belt.

• • • • • • • • • • • • 👓 • • • • • • • • • • • •

What do you sing on a Snowman's birthday?

Freeze a jolly good fellow, freeze a jolly good fellow!

What kind of car do elves drive?

Toyotas!

———————————

Why does Santa go down the chimney on Christmas Eve?

Because it soots him!

———————————

What is it called when Santa's helpers take pictures of themselves?

Elfies!

———————————

What do you call a kid who doesn't believe in Santa?

A rebel without a claus!

Why did Santa put a clock in his sleigh?

He wanted to see time fly!

What does a sheep say when it's sad on Christmas?

Baaaa humbug!

What's the most popular food in the North Pole?

Ice cream and snow cones!

How do sheep say Merry Christmas in Mexico?

¡Fleece Navidad!

Why are Christmas trees so bad at sewing?

Because they're always dropping their needles!

What does Santa pay to park his sleigh?

Nothing! It's on the house!

Where does mistletoe go to become famous?

Hollywood!

What's the best Christmas present ever?

A broken drum! You can't beat it.

How do Chihuahuas say Merry Christmas?

Fleas Navidog!

Why do mummies like Christmas so much?

Because of all the wrapping!

Why is it always so cold for Christmas?

Because it's Decembrrr!

What is a librarian's favorite Christmas song?

Silent Night!

What's the first thing Santa's helpers learn at school?

The elfabet!

What never eats at the Christmas dinner?

The turkey; it's stuffed!

Why did the Grinch go to the liquor store?

He was looking for the Holiday spirit!

What do you call a snowman with a sunburn?

A puddle.

How can you tell Santa is a gardener?

Because he ho-ho-hoes!

•·•··•··•·•• 👓 •·•··•··•··•··

How many letters are in the Christmas alphabet?

Twenty-five, because there's Noel!

•·•··•··•·•• 👓 •·•··•··•··•··

What is a snowman's favorite cereal?

Frosted Flakes!

•·•··•··•·•• 👓 •·•··•··•··•··

How do you know when Santa is in the room?

You can sense his presents!

MY JOKES

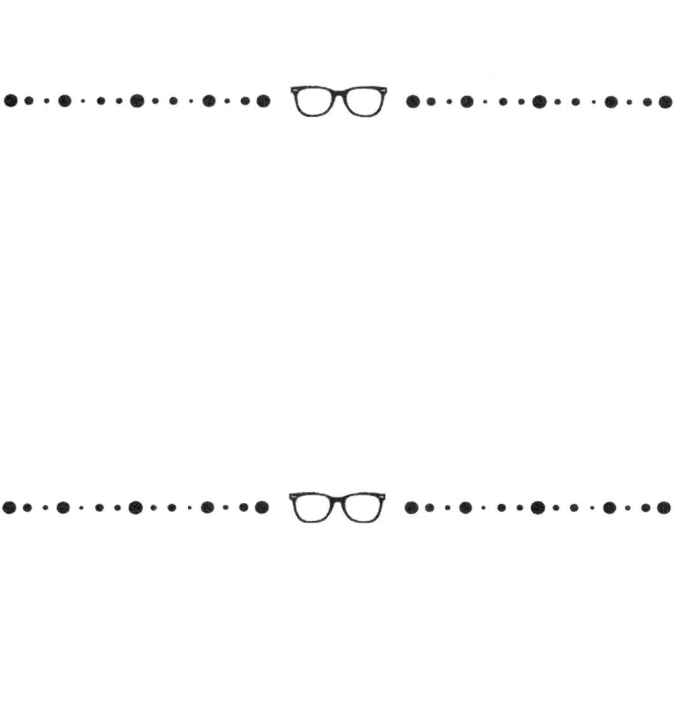

224

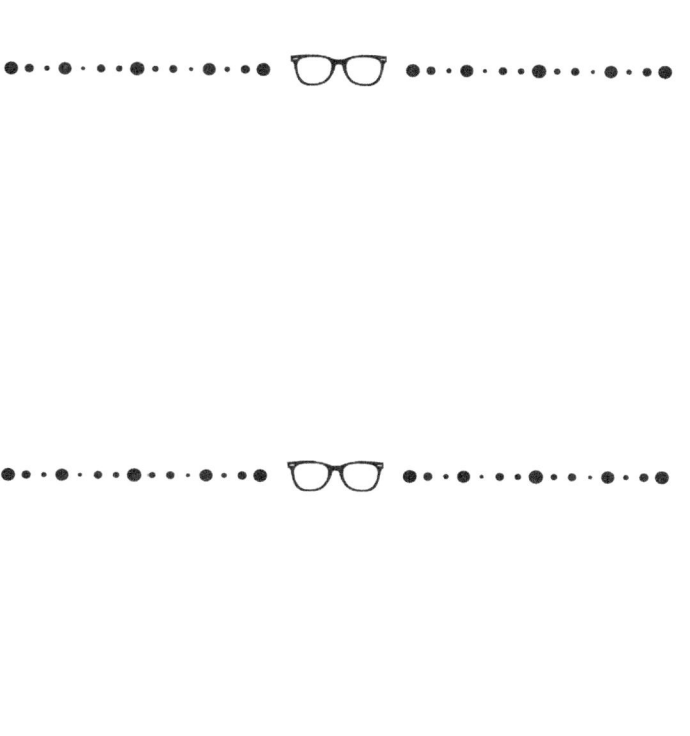

230

Printed in Dunstable, United Kingdom